THE LIFE AND LEGEND OF CHRIS KYLE

American Sniper, Navy SEAL

MICHAEL J. MOONEY

BACK BAY BOOKS
Little, Brown and Company
New York Boston London

D0029434

Back Bay Books / Little, Brown and Company
Hachette Book Group
1290 Avenue of the Americas, New York, NY 10104
littlebrown.com

Originally published as an ebook by Little, Brown and Company,
April 2013
First Back Bay paperback edition, March 2015

Back Bay Books is an imprint of Little, Brown and Company. The
Back Bay Books name and logo are trademarks of Hachette Book
Group, Inc.

The publisher is not responsible for websites (or their content)
that are not owned by the publisher.

The Hachette Speakers Bureau provides a wide range of authors
for speaking events. To find out more, go to
hachettespeakersbureau.com or call (866) 376-6591.

Portions of this book were previously published in *D Magazine*.

ISBN 978-0-316-26526-3 (pb)
LCCN 2015932605

10 9 8 7 6 5 4 3 2 1

RRD-C

Printed in the United States of America

For Tara, and for my mother

THE LIFE AND LEGEND OF CHRIS KYLE

CHAPTER 1

BEFORE THE DOORS even opened that morning, there was a line wrapped more than halfway around Cowboys Stadium, hundreds of people standing patiently, quietly, in the cold, damp air. The monolithic arena, the home of "America's Team," was the only place around that could accommodate the thousands of people who wanted to be there.

Plenty attending knew the man being memorialized that day, but most didn't. Some had read his book or seen him on television. Some had only heard of him after his death. They'd seen news reports for days, on what seemed like every channel, and had e-mailed friends and relatives they thought may not have heard yet. Families traveled from three states away. Men missed work and took their boys out of school because they thought it was important. To honor a man, to send him off the right way, to commune with fellow grievers, friends, and strangers, they came out that Monday, February 11, 2013.

The doors wouldn't open until 11:00 a.m., but some people showed up at 8:00, undeterred by the long wait. The morning was gray, thick with a fog, and it matched the somber mood in the air. When the attendants at the giant glass stadium gateways did finally open them, the crowd streamed in smoothly, silently, for hours. There was the sound of boots shuffling across the floors, of clothing rustling as people made their way in, but there were almost no words from anyone, even the stadium employees operating the metal-detecting wands. And while almost nobody spoke, nearly everyone felt some kinship, some sense of unity despite the tragedy that had brought them there that day.

There were businessmen and bikers standing

next to each other. There were college kids, young men in jeans and hunting boots, young women with their hair pinned back — all stern, stoic. There were straight-faced grandmothers who might not have otherwise left the house that day, and widows who came because their loved ones couldn't.

Most people wore black. Many wore dress uniforms. Entire teams of Navy SEALs were there, as were other special-operations fighters from multiple generations. There were police officers and sheriff's deputies and Texas Rangers. Veterans of World War II, some in wheelchairs, nodded to each other quietly as they made their way into the stadium. Some men had served in Korea, some in Vietnam, some in the first Gulf War. There were many servicemen who had never served during a war and many civilians who had never served at all, but they all felt compelled to come.

The mass of people wanted to be there for him, for this American hero, because he had been there for them. He had always given everything for his family, for his friends, for his SEAL teammates. He'd been there for strangers who needed help, for countrymen who needed protection. The people who had never met him needed to show him how much he meant to them, too. They needed to make a statement, to honor something bigger than themselves. They came out because they agreed with what he stood for, what he lived for, and both what he was — a loyal family man, a fearsome combatant, an outspoken patriot — and what he symbolized: an American with American ideals.

These past few years have been rough for so many people. Nobody can remember a time when there has been such uncertainty in this country, such serious doubts about the future of the United States of America. So much of our collective recent past has been defined by grid-lock, disagreement, disingenuousness — fears of all kinds. There have been drastic social changes, fundamental policy shifts, economic struggles, and that sustained, residual dread of terrorism. Even sports — what used to be an escape from the seriousness of life for so many people — has been filled with stories about cheaters and scandals and fallen demigods who once seemed pristine and sacred. Now no sports page would be complete without the words *testosterone* or *concussion* and a quote from a press conference somewhere in there.

So many Americans have been searching, grasping for someone, something to believe in. People have needed a hero. People have needed an icon, someone larger than life, like the heroes in history books and in movies. They have needed someone strong but humble, someone modest. Someone courageous, self-sacrificing, willing to go and do what the rest of us can't or won't. Someone smart, someone spiritual. Someone fighting for good, fighting against evil, fighting for freedom and for something bigger.

The people who came out that day were there because they'd found a hero fitting that description. He was American to the core, a highly trained warrior brought up to love God and country — the kind of man about whom ha-

giographies are written. He was a Texan, a cowboy. He was hope, assurance, the face of security,
the epitome of fidelity. He was the proof that
real-life superheroes walk among us, that some
men are more than mere mortals. He was the
broad chest and the cold eyes. Even before he
died, he was already as close as anyone in modern times has come to being a living, breathing
mythological figure.

He was already a legend.

CHAPTER 2

THERE'S A STORY about Chris Kyle: On a cold January morning in 2010, he pulled into a gas station somewhere along Route 67, south of Dallas. He was driving his supercharged black Ford F-350 outfitted with black rims and oversize knobby mudding tires. Kyle had replaced the Ford logo on the grill with a small chrome skull, similar to the Punisher emblem from the Marvel Comics series, and added a riot-ready aftermarket grill guard bearing the words ROAD ARMOR. He had just left the Navy and moved back to Texas, and he was simply putting some gas in his truck.

Two guys approached him with pistols and demanded his money and his keys. With his hands in the air, he sized up which man seemed most confident with his gun.

Kyle knew what confidence with a gun looked like. He was the deadliest sniper in American history. He had at least 160 confirmed kills by the Pentagon's count, but by his own count — and the estimates of his Navy SEAL teammates — the number was closer to twice that. In his four tours of duty in Iraq, Kyle earned two Silver Stars and five Bronze Stars with Valor. He survived six improvised explosive device (IED) attacks, three gunshot wounds, two helicopter crashes, and more surgeries than he could remember. He was known among his SEAL brethren as The Legend and to his enemies as *al-shaitan*, "the devil."

He told the robbers that he just needed to grab the keys from the truck. He turned around and reached under his winter coat instead, into his waistband. With his right hand, he grabbed his Colt 1911. He fired two shots under his left armpit, hitting the first man twice in the chest. Then he turned slightly and fired two more times, hitting the second man twice in the chest. Both men fell dead.

Kyle leaned on his truck and waited for the police.

When they arrived, they detained him while running his driver's license. But instead of his name, address, and date of birth, what came up was a phone number at the Department of Defense. The officers called, and at the other end of the line was someone who explained that they were in the presence of one of the most skilled fighters in U.S. military history. When they reviewed the surveillance footage, the officers found the incident had happened just as Kyle had described it. They were very understanding, and they didn't want to drag a recently home, highly decorated veteran into a messy legal situation.

Kyle wasn't unnerved or bothered. Quite the opposite. He'd been feeling depressed since he left the service, struggling to adjust to civilian life. This was an exciting reminder of the action he missed.

That night, talking on the phone to his wife, Taya — who was in the process of moving with their kids from California — he was a good husband. He asked how her day was. The way some people tell it, he got caught up in their conversation and only right before they hung up did he remember his big news of the day: "Oh yeah, I shot two guys trying to steal my truck today."

A brief description of the incident appeared in fellow SEAL Marcus Luttrell's 2012 book, *Service: A Navy SEAL at War* — but not in Kyle's own bestseller, *American Sniper* — and there are mentions of it in various forums deep in the corners of the internet. Before Kyle's murder at the hands of a fellow veteran in February, I asked him about that story during an interview in his office last year. It was part of what was supposed to be an extended, in-depth magazine story about his service and how hard he had worked to adjust back to this world — to become the great husband and father and Christian he'd always wanted to be.

He didn't want to get into the specifics about the gas station shooting, but after sitting across a table from him talking about it generally, I left that day believing it had happened.

CHAPTER 3

THE DALLAS OFFICES of Craft International, the defense contractor where Chris Kyle was president until his death, were immaculate when I visited him. You needed one of the broad-chested security guards from downstairs as an escort just to get to that floor of the building. Sitting under thick glass in the lobby, there was an exceptionally rare original English translation of Galileo's *Dialogue* (circa 1661) about the sun, the earth, and which revolved around the other. A conference room held a safe full of gigantic guns — guns illegal to own without a Department of Defense contract.

At thirty-eight, Kyle was a large man, six foot

two, 230 pounds, and the muscles in his neck, shoulders, and forearms made him seem even bigger, like a scruffy-bearded giant. When he greeted me with a direct look in the eye and a firm handshake, his huge bear paw enveloped my hand. That day he had on boots, jeans, a black T-shirt, and a baseball cap. It's the same thing he wore most days he came to the office, or when he watched his daughter's ballet recitals, or during television interviews with Conan O'Brien or Bill O'Reilly.

This was one of the rare chances when he'd have a few hours to talk. Over the next three days, he would be teaching a sniper course to the Dallas SWAT teams and had three book signings, one at a hospital in Tyler (for a terminal cancer patient whose doctor reached out to Kyle), one at Ray's Sporting Goods in Dallas, and one at the VA Hospital in Fort Worth. He'd also have to fly down to Austin for a shooting event Craft was putting on for Speaker of the House John Boehner and several other congressmen.

"We are not doing this for free," he said, anticipating a question. "We accept Republicans and Democrats alike, as long as the money is good."

A few weeks later, he would have to cancel a weekend meeting with me because he was invited to hang out with George W. Bush. "Sorry," he said when asked if anyone else might be able to join. "Not even my wife's allowed to come."

Chris Kyle loved the Dallas Cowboys and the University of Texas Longhorns. He loved going to the Alamo, looking at historic artifacts. The license plate on his truck had a picture of the flag used during the Texas Revolution, depicting a cannon, a star, and the words COME AND TAKE IT. Being in the military forced him to move a lot, and neither of his children was born in Texas. But for each birth, he had his family send a box of dirt from home — so that the first ground his child's foot touched would be Texas soil.

He would often apologize to Vietnam veterans or their children for the way servicemen were treated when they first came back from war, even though he hadn't even been born at the time.

He was outspoken on a lot of issues. He believed strongly in the Second Amendment, politely decrying the "incredible stupidity" of gun control laws anytime he was asked. He said he was hesitant to see the movie *Zero Dark Thirty* because he'd heard that it was a lot of propaganda for the Obama administration. On the night of the 2012 presidential election, he posted to his tens of thousands of Facebook fans: "Wow. I didn't know there would be so many stupid people in this country. Oh well, better buckle up. It's going to be a bumpy ride to socialism."

When Bob Costas discussed gun control during a football game, Kyle took to Facebook to contradict him. "FOOL!" he wrote. "If you are gonna hold the gun responsible for killing a person, then you need to hold the spoon responsible for making Rosie O'Donnell fat!"

Around the same time, he posted this: "If you don't like what I have to say or post, you forget one thing, I don't give a shit what you think. LOL."

He didn't worry about sounding politically incorrect. The Craft International company slogan, emblazoned around the Punisher skull on the logo, reads, "Despite what your momma told you, violence does solve problems."

His views were nuanced, though. "If you hate the war, that's fine," he told me. "But you should still support the troops. They don't get to pick where they're deployed. They just gave the American people a blank check for anything up to and including the value of their lives, and the least everyone else can do is be thankful. Buy them dinner. Mow their yard. Bake them cookies."

"The best way to describe Chris," his wife, Taya, says, "is 'extremely multifaceted.'"

He was a brutal warrior but a gentle father and husband. He was a patient instructor, and he was a persistent, sophomoric jokester. If he had access to your Facebook account, he might announce to all your friends and family that you're gay and finally coming out of the closet. If he really wanted to make you squirm, he might get hold of your phone and scroll through your photos threatening to see if you kept naked pictures of your girlfriend. And if you took any of it too seriously, you might face the risk of getting lovingly choked out.

There was a party trick he liked to perform, a sleeper hold that would render a man unconscious in seconds. Kyle called it a "hug." It started in high school and didn't stop. Eventually, by the time he was a national hero, people would dare him to do it to them, saying they wouldn't go down.

Kyle could also be kind beyond measure: giving away 100 percent of his share of the proceeds from his book, for instance. Or offering to let mothers of his fallen SEAL teammates live in his home. Or sitting for hours with an annoying, awed reporter — then inviting him to tag along and observe his life for a few days.

We had originally focused on me writing a story about his transition, the strange journey from the sniper picking off targets to the suburban T-ball coach. He'd done a lot of interviews and seemed so complex, so interesting from a journalistic standpoint. It wasn't just about reconciling the killing and the kindness. He seemed to have readjusted to civilian life so well at a time when so many were struggling. He seemed to bear the mantle that comes along with being a celebrated war hero reluctantly but graciously.

His story had meaning politically, socially, historically. But it also excited the child inside of me. This was a man who'd been described as a "real-life G.I. Joe." Right there, a few feet away from where we sat at Craft, were the kind of giant guns you only see in high-budget action movies. And with his throaty Texas accent, he would answer any question I could come up with.

Kyle liked when people thought of him as a dumb hillbilly, since he actually had a remarkable ability to retain information, whether it was a mission briefing, the details of a business meeting, or his encyclopedic knowledge of his own hero, Vietnam-era Marine sniper Carlos Hathcock. While on the sniper rifle, Kyle, a former bronco buster, had to do complicated math, accounting for the speed of the wind, the spin of a bullet (he could explain the Coriolis effect better than a lot of science teachers), and the curvature of the earth — and he had to do it quickly, under the most intense pressure imaginable. Those were the moments when he thrived.

The most common question he was asked was easy for him to answer. He said he never regretted any of his kills, which weren't all men.

"I regret the people I couldn't kill before they got to my boys," he said. That's how he referred to the men and women he served with, across the branches: "my boys."

He said he didn't enjoy killing, but he did like protecting Americans and allies and civilians. He was the angel of death, sprawled flat atop a roof, his University of Texas Longhorns ball cap turned backward as he picked off enemy targets one by one before they could hurt his boys. He was the guardian, assigned to watch over open-air street markets and elections, the places that might make good marks for insurgent terrorists.

"You don't think of the people you kill as people," he said. "They're just targets. You can't think of them as people with families and jobs. They rule by putting terror in the hearts of innocent people. The things they would do — beheadings, dragging Americans through the streets alive — the things they would do to little boys and women just to keep them terrified and quiet" — he paused for a moment and slowed down. "That part is easy. I definitely don't have any regrets about that."

He said he didn't feel like a hero. "I'm just a regular guy. I just did a job. I was in some badass situations, but it wasn't just me. My teammates made it possible." He gave all the credit to his training, to the military. He matter-of-factly explained that he just so happened to come across more targets that fit the very narrow rules of engagement. He wasn't the best sniper in the SEAL teams, he said. "I'm probably middle of the pack. I was just in the right spots at the right times."

The way he saw it, the most difficult thing he ever did was getting out of the Navy.

"I left knowing the guy who replaced me," he

said. "If he dies, or if he messes up and other people die, that's on me. You really feel like you're letting down these guys you've gone through hell with."

The hardest part of leaving the service? "Missing my boys. Missing being around them in the action. That's your whole life, every day for years. I hate to say it, but when you're back and you're just walking around a mall or something, you feel like a pussy." It nagged at him. "You hear someone whining about something at a stoplight, and it's like, Man, three weeks ago I was getting shot at, and you're complaining about — I don't even care what."

There was also the struggle to readjust to his family life. "When I got out, I realized I barely knew my kids," he said. "I barely knew my wife. In the three years before I got out, I spent a total of six months at home. It's hard to go from God, Country, Family to God, Family, Country."

But three years after he left the SEALs, he had a job he liked. He could do (mildly) badass things: shoot big guns, detonate an occasional string of explosives, be around a lot of other former special-operations types. His marriage was finally back in a good place. He had a book on the bestseller list. And he had the chance to help veterans through a number of charities.

"A lot of these guys just miss being around their boys, too," he said. "They need guys who speak their speak. They don't need to be treated like they're special."

He'd often take vets out to the gun range. Being around people who understood what they'd been through, being able to relax and shoot off some rounds, it was a little like group therapy.

With his family, and with training people, helping people, he had found a new purpose. Chris Kyle could do anything if he had a purpose. He'd been like that since he was a little boy.

CHAPTER 4

HE WAS THE son of a church deacon and a Sunday-school teacher. His father's job at Southwestern Bell had the family moving a lot, and though he was born in Odessa, he told people he grew up "all over Texas." Both parents kept busy and worked hard: his father always maintained two jobs, and his mother went back to work as soon as the boys left the house. Kyle had two dreams as a little boy: he wanted to be a cowboy, and he wanted to be a Marine.

Guns were part of life. When he was little, he played with BB guns: a Daisy pump rifle and a CO_2-powered revolver designed to look like the 1860 model Colt Peacemaker. When he was eight years old, his father gave him his first real gun. About the same time he was learning to read, he was learning to shoot. Little Chris had a bolt-action .30-06 that he later admitted scared him a bit, and his younger brother, Jeff, had a Marlin .30-30 with a cowboy-style lever-action. They liked to go hunting with their father, but animals weren't the only thing they hunted.

For his birthday parties, Kyle liked to have BB-gun wars. It's actually quite common in Texas. Boys descend on a neighborhood or a park and pretend to be enemies. He would perch on the roof of his parents' house, waiting for his friends to dart across the yard. He wasn't a great shot back then, but at least one friend is still walking around with one of Kyle's BBs in his hand.

Jeff was born four years after Chris. He always had a slightly smaller build, and his brown hair made the older brother's strawberry-blond mop seem even lighter. The family has dozens of photos that show the young boys growing up together. If they shared a cupcake and Chris came away with frosting on his face, his brother did, too. As Jeff got older, he would ride a small bicycle designed to look like a police motorcycle. While Jeff gripped the handlebars, Chris would push him along, the older brother's eyes fixed on the horizon, the sides of his little mouth curled just a bit.

There's a picture of Chris at around nine or ten years old, dressed in a number 33 Tony Dorsett Dallas Cowboys uniform, replete with a small white helmet and chinstrap. He's looking out from the helmet grinning, baring his teeth. Beside him is Jeff, in an even smaller version of the same number 33 uniform, the too-big-by-far helmet askew on his young head.

Their parents would let them box each other in the family living room. Chris didn't go easy on the younger sibling, and standing there with one hand behind his back — because that was the rule — and one gloved fist up, he was ready to strike like a rattlesnake. Jeff wouldn't back down either, flinging both of his tiny hands at his brother without fear. Later, he'd explain their dynamic to reporters like this: "We pulled each other's chains all the time, and pushed each other's buttons, definitely."

That's the way the big brother liked it. He was ceaselessly competitive, but he never wanted his younger brother to quit. Being strong, being rugged, was a virtue in the Kyle household from very early on. Developing internal strength was as important as developing muscles, a lesson re-inforced every time they watched an old Western or a war movie, when the family sat around the dinner table, and every weekend at church.

The brothers were inseparable for years. "His brother was his best friend," Taya says. They would go target shooting together in the woods. As they grew up, they worked on ranches to-gether, competed in rodeos together, and would eventually join the military around the same time. Jeff went into the Marines the way the older brother had always talked about.

During high school in Midlothian, Kyle played football and baseball. He showed cows with the FFA. He and his buddies cruised for girls in nearby Waxahachie. Bryan Rury was a close friend of Kyle's in high school. Rury was much smaller, but it seemed they were always standing next to each other. "I think Chris liked looking like a giant," Rury says.

Kyle certainly had a devilish streak, but he was also, generally, a good kid. One time he found Rury smoking a cigarette. "He threatened to tell my mother," Rury says. "He just kept saying, 'Do you know how stupid that is? Do you? Why would you do something stupid like that?'"

Once when he was a senior, in the halls during a class period for some reason, he saw a younger kid, a freshman, crying against the wall. When the younger student saw the senior — a big, popular kid at the top of the high school social hierarchy — the freshman tried to mask his tears. But Kyle still stopped. He turned to the kid, looked him in the eye, and said, simply, "Hey, I cry sometimes, too."

If that doesn't sound like a lot, you've never been a freshman who felt lonely. It's the kind of story his friends would recount when trying to describe how he could be simultaneously gruff and genuinely sweet. The same person who would stop and help a kid he didn't know pick up a pile of dropped schoolbooks would be on the playground fighting later that day.

He liked to fight. Or rather, the way his friends describe it, he was just really, really good at it. Once someone gave a solid shove or threw a punch, Kyle would be all over him. He could turn so fast and hit so hard, fights rarely lasted beyond the first few seconds.

"When you're a kid, and you're really good at something, you just like doing it," Rury says. "And nobody was as good at anything as Chris was at fighting."

His father warned him never to start a fight. Kyle said he lived by that code "most of the time." He found that if he was sticking up for his friends, or for kids who couldn't defend themselves, he got to fight and he got to be the good guy at the same time. Once he felt like he was standing up for something right, he would never back down.

One time, there was a new kid in school who was trying to make a name for himself by picking on Rury. Kyle came into class one day to find Rury quiet, upset. "He asked me what was wrong, and I wouldn't tell him," Rury says. "But he figured it out on his own pretty fast."

Kyle went over to the new kid's desk and, in his not-so-subtle Chris Kyle way, told him he better leave his friend alone. Or else. The kid stood up from his desk and they went at it. While Kyle almost never started the fight, his friends say, he always ended it. "As they were taking him off to the principal's office, I just remember him flashing me that giant smile of his," Rury says.

That grin could mean many things. It might mean he was having fun, like when he was with horses or guns. It might mean he was happy to be with his friends or family, hanging out and cracking jokes. If it was that mischievous, devilish smile, it meant someone was about to be on the receiving end of a practical joke — or about to get choked unconscious.

After high school, Rury says, they didn't talk

33

that often. But more than fifteen years later, when Kyle eventually quit the Navy and moved back to Texas, they picked up right where they'd left off.

"It was like we didn't miss a day," Rury says. "He would just call me up some afternoons and ask if I wanted to stop by the house and hang out." They'd get together for beers and sit and talk. "He was that same person," Rury says. "No matter how big or famous he got. He was the same friend from when I was ten. He'd be totally honest when you needed to hear it. Sometimes if I was complaining or feeling uptight he'd just say, 'Bryan, I love you, but you're being a little bitch right now.' Then we'd be totally fine. That's a true friend."

CHAPTER 5

GROWING UP ON small ranches meant that working with animals was part of life. On weekends the boys fed the horses, moved cattle, and inspected the fence lines. Kyle would tell stories about punching cows in the head out of frustration and, by his record, twice breaking his hand. By contrast, he said he would never hit a horse. He felt like they were smarter than cattle, that it was more of a cooperative interaction. This, he would later explain, is what gave him the patience he needed as a sniper.

He also rode bulls in small local rodeo competitions. He essentially taught himself, and he didn't win much, though he enjoyed the lifestyle:

the traveling and partying, the manly exertion and the occasional "buckle bunny." It all made him feel like a real cowboy.

After high school, he went to Tarleton State University, mostly to postpone the responsibilities of adulthood, and he continued to enter riding competitions — broncos or bulls — anytime he had the chance. But during his freshman year, his rodeo career came to an end. He was in a starting chute in Rendon, Texas, on top of a bronco when it bucked and flipped on him, knocking him out. The way Kyle told it, the horse had come down on him awkwardly, and the cowboys had to essentially roll the animal back over him to open the chute. When it was over, Kyle had a dislocated shoulder, a broken rib, a bruised lung and kidney, and a set of pins in both of his wrists.

In his book, he would talk about how a few weeks later he was on a date with a girl he liked when the screws sticking out of either side of both wrists — he compared them to the neck bolts of Frankenstein's monster — started bothering him. So he broke one of them off at the base with his bare hands.

"I don't guess she was too impressed with that," he wrote. "The date ended early."

When he told me the story, he lifted his giant hands up to show me the spot, as close to supplicating as he ever got.

"Right here," he said, pointing at the side of his right wrist.

In college, he spent more time drinking than studying, and soon he decided he'd rather be working on a ranch full time and considered trying to work his way up to the job of ranch manager one day. He loved the work, sweating in the sobering sun, feeling that special blend of accomplishment and exhaustion at the end of the day. But he knew his future was in the military — in the Marines, he thought — and he figured he shouldn't waste any more time.

The Marine recruiting office is right next to the Army, Navy, and Air Force offices. As luck would have it, the day Kyle showed up to enlist, the Marine recruiter was out of the office for lunch. But the other recruiters were there — waiting, inviting. He compared the recruiters to snipers themselves, picking off targets as they walked down the hall.

The first recruiter to get to him was from the Army. Kyle heard all about the Army's Special Forces. He heard about the Rangers, and about jumping from planes and small-arms training. Then came the Navy, where he heard about the SEALs, and how competitive and challenging their preliminary school would be.

He was more than intrigued. He said that at that moment, he wanted to be a SEAL more than anything. So much so that when the recruiter told him he would have a better chance of making the teams if he rejected his signing bonus — something Kyle realized later probably made the recruiter look pretty good to his bosses — he didn't think twice and declined the money.

With just a small twist of fate, a slight variance in the lunch scheduling of a stranger, the arc of his life could have been completely different.

If he had become a Marine, who knows where it would have taken him, or how well-suited he would have been to the challenges. Who knows how many people would have ever known the name Chris Kyle. Perhaps his will to win and his ability to fight and to thrive under pressure would have driven him in the same way. Maybe he would have decided it wasn't for him and dropped it early on.

I asked him if he ever thought about how his life could have been so different. If he ever wondered how it might have played out if maybe the Marine recruiter had brought his lunch to work that day.

Kyle said he rarely considered it. After that day in the Navy recruiter's office, it didn't matter. He didn't want to be a Marine anymore. Now, he wanted to be a SEAL.

There was a problem, though. Kyle still had pins in his arm from the rodeo accident, and when he took the physical required at the beginning of BUD/S (Basic Underwater Demolition/SEAL) training, he was told he'd be disqualified, that he would never even have a chance to compete.

So he quit school for good and focused on being a full-time rancher in Colorado. After working in the cold for months — and missing the heat of Texas — he was arranging to move back when he got a call from a Navy recruiter, asking if he still wanted to be a SEAL. Within days, he was ready to go. He had been a cowboy, was done with it. It was time for the other half of his dream to begin.

CHAPTER 6

KYLE BREEZED THROUGH the Navy's basic training. He only made it through BUD/S training by way of sheer resolve. He told stories about lying there on the beach, his arms linked with his friends', their heads hovering above the frigid rising tide. He knew if he got up and rang the bell — if he quit — he could get hot coffee and a doughnut. The uncontrollable shivering — they called it "jackhammering" — lasted for hours, but he never wanted to stop. He joked that he was only lazy, that if the bell had been a little closer, maybe his entire life would have been different. But the truth is, nothing could have kept him from his dream.

"He had more willpower than anyone I've ever met," Taya says. "If he cared about something, he just wouldn't ever quit. You can't fail at something if you just never quit."

Taya met Kyle in a bar just after he finished BUD/S training. She lived in Long Beach at the time and was going through a dark patch of life in a new town when a friend invited her to San Diego for a night out somewhere different. She resisted at first — San Diego was 90 minutes away — and then again when the bar her friend liked had a cover charge. But she went in anyway and was standing with her friend when this short-haired, muscle-bound Texan approached her. When she asked what he did — she suspected from the physique and the swagger that he was in the military — he initially told her he drove an ice cream truck. (He'd told other women he was a "dolphin waxer.") She figured he'd be arrogant but was surprised to find him idealistic instead. But she was still skeptical. Taya's sister had divorced a guy who was trying to become a SEAL, and

Taya had specifically stated she could never marry someone like that.

They stayed and talked for hours, she remembers, both of them mostly ignoring their respective friends. Finally Taya gave in and passed him her phone number. Then, after last call, they walked out to the parking lot — and Taya promptly vomited up the scotch she'd been drinking all night.

Taya grew up in Oregon, the youngest daughter of a small-town mayor. She's petite, with soft brunette hair and dark eyes that can turn fierce in a split second. She's hard, cynical, and very protective of her two children. (Before agreeing to an interview with me, she sent her friend, a member of the Dallas SWAT unit, to feel me out and make sure I was who I claimed to be.) She had to be independent and strong, especially to be with a Navy SEAL.

Kyle turned out to be quite sensitive. He was able to read her better than anyone she'd known. Even when she thought she was keeping something hidden behind a good facade, he could always see through it. That kept them from needing to talk about their emotions or constantly reassess their relationship. They didn't need to get, as Taya would put it later, "all feely and dramatic," and that suited her. When they were together, life felt easier for both of them, she says. They got married shortly before he shipped out to Iraq for the first time.

CHAPTER 7

IT TAKES YEARS to earn enough trust to be a SEAL sniper. Even after sniper school, Kyle had to prove himself again and again in the field, under the pressure of battle. He served other missions before going to Afghanistan and Iraq, in places he couldn't discuss because the operations were classified.

As he would eventually describe in *American Sniper*, his first kill on the rifle came in late March 2003, in Nasiriyah, Iraq. It wasn't long after the initial invasion, and his platoon — "Charlie" of SEAL Team 3 — had taken a building earlier that day so they could provide overwatch for a unit of Marines thundering down the road. He was holding a bolt-action .300 Winchester Magnum that belonged to his platoon chief. He saw a woman about fifty yards away. As the Marines got closer, the woman pulled a grenade. Hollywood might have you believe that snipers aim for the head — "one shot, one kill" — but effective snipers aim for the middle of the chest, for center mass.

Kyle pulled the trigger twice.

"The public is soft," he used to say. "They have no idea." Because of that softness, he had to have that story, and others, cleared by the Department of Defense before he could include them in his book.

He wanted outsiders to know exactly what kind of evil the troops have to deal with. But he understood why the Pentagon wouldn't want to give America's enemies any new propaganda. He knew the public didn't want to hear about the brutal realities of war.

Kyle served four tours of duty in Iraq, participating in every major campaign of the war. He was on the ground for the initial invasion in 2003.

He was in Fallujah in 2004. He went back, to Ramadi in 2006, and then again, to Baghdad in 2008, where he was called in to secure the Green Zone by going into Sadr City.

Most of his platoon was stationed in the Pacific before their 2004 deployment to Iraq. Kyle was sent early to assist Marines with clearing insurgents in Fallujah. Tales of his success in combat trickled back to his team. He was originally supposed to watch over the American forces perched at a safe distance, but he thought he could provide more protection if he was on the street, going house to house with his boys. During one firefight, it was reported that Kyle ran through a hail of bullets to pull a wounded Marine to safety. It was then that his teammates, hearing these stories, started sarcastically referring to him as The Legend.

Those tales of bravery in battle proliferated upon his third deployment. A younger SEAL was with Kyle at the top of a building in Ramadi when they came under heavy fire. The younger SEAL, who is still active in the teams and can't be named, dropped to the ground and hid behind an interior wall. When he finally looked up, he saw Kyle standing there, glued to his weapon, covering his field of fire, calling out enemy positions as he engaged.

When he was on the sniper rifle, Kyle was almost always in a defensive position. If he set up in an abandoned house, he'd have at least until he fired his first shot before his position was exposed. If he and his group had to take over an occupied house as a temporary home base, they'd have to feed the family and take them to the restroom, but they couldn't let the family members leave the house. So when nobody came out in the morning, the neighbors always knew that Americans were there, and it would be a matter of time before the enemy knew, too.

In the bulk of the war, snipers were used to make precision kills in the middle of the battlefield. They were an alternative to methods used in other wars, where resistance would have been countered largely by artillery, close-range machine guns, and other weapons that could destroy large swaths of a city and inevitably kill a large number of civilians. (For recent examples, look at the tactics employed by the Syrian government during the ongoing civil war there.) The strict rules of modern engagement essentially turned American soldiers into bait for the enemy. That was true for the snipers as well as the men on the ground they were supposed to protect. The enemy responded to the bait, and firefights ensued.

Kyle said combat was the worst on his final deployment, to Sadr City in 2008. The enemy was better armed than before. Now it seemed as if every time there was an attack, there were rocket-propelled grenades (RPGs) and fights that went on for days. This was also the deployment that produced Kyle's longest-distance confirmed kill.

He was on the second floor of a house on the edge of a village. Using the scope of his .338 Lapua, he began to scan farther out into the distance, to the edge of the next village, a mile away. He saw a figure on the roof of a one-story building. The figure didn't seem to be doing much, and at the moment he didn't appear to have a weapon. But later that day, as an Army convoy approached, Kyle checked again and saw the man holding what looked like an RPG. At that distance, Kyle could only estimate his calculations.

He pulled the trigger and watched through his scope as the Iraqi, 2,100 yards away, fell off the roof. It was the world's eighth-longest confirmed kill by a sniper. Later, Kyle called it a "really, really lucky shot."

One of the things that surprised me most when I was interviewing him was just how much Kyle knew about American snipers of yesteryear. I had done some research into snipers of the past, including Carlos Hathcock. But as Kyle and I talked, it became clear that he knew Hathcock's story down to the last detail. He had read at least two books that focused completely on the famed Vietnam-era sniper, and when I emailed him a long newspaper profile of Hathcock from the 1980s, he eagerly read that, too. As it turned out, Chris Kyle, the most publicized war hero in decades, had a hero of his own.

Most of Hathcock's kills came in jungles, from covered positions in the damp mulch and climbing ferns. His most famous strike — one that would later become lore, talked about in bars and American Legion halls, depicted in several movies and books and articles — came against a North Vietnamese sniper. They'd been hunting each other for days. Hathcock, lying still and silent, flat on his stomach in the mud, gnats digging at the corners of his eyes and the creases of his mouth, spotted a glint of light coming off some leaves across a clearing. He lined up his scope and fired — only later learning that the bullet went straight through the North Vietnamese soldier's scope and into his eye.

Kyle admired the skills required for one-on-one hunting, the adrenaline and thrill that must have come with that particular kind of targeting. He called Hathcock "the greatest sniper that ever lived." He knew all about the various missions his hero had gone on, about the weapons he'd used. And he knew about the way Hathcock — along with so many other veterans from that time — was treated when he got home, how civilians and activists saw him as a ruthless, cold-blooded killer.

Back then snipers were viewed as cowards by a lot of society. The idea was this: anyone who could look through a scope and see a person up close — the tiny hairs on a target's neck, the flare of someone's nostrils, the things that make you remember a person's individuality — anyone who could see all that and still pull the trigger must be soulless.

Kyle would point out that snipers, especially in urban warfare, decrease the number of civilian casualties. Sniper teams are generally pinpoint strikers, their jobs the combat equivalent of a scalpel cut. Plus, he said, "I will reach out and get you however I can if you're threatening American lives."

Many details of Kyle's life story resembled Hathcock's, actually. There was the obvious: Both men were known for extraordinarily high numbers of confirmed kills. (Hathcock had ninety-three by the military's count, though it was likely much higher.) Both of them had nicknames — Hathcock was known as White Feather for the tiny bit of bravado he kept tucked into the band of his bush hat, Kyle as The Legend. And like Kyle, Hathcock told people that he didn't feel like a hero. In the old newspaper story I had showed Kyle, Hathcock is quoted, saying, "It was just a job."

There were little details their stories had in common. Both had a war anecdote that involved a run-in with a snake, for example. And then there were deeper similarities: They both grew up hunting in the woods as boys. Hathcock was from Arkansas, not so unlike Texas in many ways. Both watched Westerns and war movies as kids and dreamed of serving in the military even before they could. Hathcock, too, volunteered for multiple tours, going back even when the war had become incredibly unpopular. Each talked about killing a woman while on the sniper rifle — for both it was with two shots — and

Hathcock also told people that he didn't regret any of his kills.

Both men were bitter when they eventually had to leave the service. Both credited their wives with helping them get through the darkest times. Both later wrote books about their experiences as snipers, and because the American public has always found the topic fascinating, both became relatively well known for their service. But both also felt like the public would simply never be able to understand the stark, harsh realities of modern war.

CHAPTER 8

CHRIS KYLE DIDN'T fit the stereotype of the sullen, lone-wolf sniper. By all accounts, his cackling laugh was a staple during training missions, and sometimes during combat as well. In many ways, he was far from the model serviceman. While he always kept his weapons clean, the same was not true of his living space. The way some SEALs tell it, after one deployment his room was in such a disgusting condition that it took two days to clean. Around the bed there were six months' worth of spent sunflower seed shells he had spit out.

There are also tales of the nights when his platoon would return from a mission, and as everyone else went off to bed, Chris Kyle would choose instead to play video games, firing up his computer for an epic session of *Madden* football. While the intensity of combat exhausted most of his teammates, he sometimes found it invigorating. He could stay up all night.

He was seldom seen in anything remotely resembling a military uniform. His teammates remember him painting the Punisher skull on his body armor, helmets, and even his guns. He also cut the sleeves off his shirts. He wore civilian hunting shoes instead of combat boots. Eschewing the protection of Kevlar headgear, he wore his old Longhorns baseball cap. He told people he wore the hat so that the enemy knew Texas was represented, that "Texans shoot straight."

Kyle terrorized his enemies in true folk-hero fashion. In 2006, intelligence officers reported there was a $20,000 bounty on his head. Before long it went up to $80,000. He would explain later that the bounties were probably for any snipers, as the enemy would have no reliable way to differentiate individual American snipers —

but that's how legends work. Kyle knew that by making his name and face known, he was also standing in and representing all the warriors the public didn't know. He knew that figure, $80,000, represented to people the real risks, dangers, and overlying pressures American troops felt. At one point he even joked that he was afraid to go home: "I was worried my wife might turn me in."

Taya has been asked often over the years how she reconciles the two Chris Kyles, the trained killer and the loving husband and father — the man who rolled around on the floor with his kids, planned vacations to historical sites, and called from wherever he could. Once, he thought his phone was off and Taya ended up overhearing a firefight. She always worried about him, but understanding how he could do what he did was never hard.

"Chris was out there fighting for his brothers because he loved them," she says. "He wanted to protect them and make sure they all got to go home to their families."

Nobody needed to ask him why he signed up for the military, why he decided to sign over everything up to and including the value of his life. There's a quote from his book that made its way around the internet. It sums up his feelings: "I've lived the literal meaning of the 'land of the free' and 'home of the brave.' It's not corny for me. I feel it in my heart. I feel it in my chest. Even at a ball game, when someone talks during the anthem or doesn't take off his hat, it pisses me off." He added, with that Chris Kyle charm, "I'm not one to be quiet about it, either."

But he noticed that the Iraqis the U.S. forces were training didn't feel the same way. He couldn't talk with me about exactly what kind of training he was involved with or witnessed, but he said he could see that the Iraqi troops just weren't patriotic. They weren't passionate about building a disciplined military, he'd say. What's more, Kyle would tell people that he didn't blame those troops either.

"They don't love their country," he would explain.

He never cared to talk much about the number of confirmed kills he had. By all accounts, it's considerably higher than what the Pentagon has released publicly, but certain records could remain classified for decades. When he was eventually convinced to sit down and write a book, the number was discussed quite a bit. Jim DeFelice cowrote *American Sniper* with Kyle. He says this topic came up a lot early in the process.

"There is an 'official' number of kills that is fairly well known inside the SEAL community," DeFelice says. "It's higher than what we use in the book. That figure was purposely ambiguous — the words 'more than' were specifically chosen to satisfy both the truth and objections from the military that using the real number would lead to revelations about classified information."

The author says they spent a lot of time going over how Kyle felt about using the number, and those discussions are detailed in the beginning of the book. "While his thoughts and feelings on the subject went back and forth," DeFelice says, "I think in his heart of hearts he always preferred not using any number at all. The number really doesn't express what his story was, though it did bring people to the story."

DeFelice explained how snipers keep track of such things. "We know the number because, very early on, his command began keeping extremely detailed reports on the battlefield," he says. "There was literally someone taking notes not just on every kill, but every shot snipers took, even in the middle of combat."

But even the official number, DeFelice says, is almost certainly less than the actual total number of men Kyle killed in combat. "It doesn't include combatants who died out of sight or couldn't otherwise be confirmed as KIA (killed in action) — who were shot and retreated around a corner, only to die there," he says. "The number also doesn't include action during a number of missions that remain classified. None of those missions are described in the book, nor was there ever an intention to do so."

Of course, the mere discussion, the quantifying of death in such ways, feels macabre. The "number" has generated a lot of controversy. "I think a certain percentage of people are appalled by it," DeFelice says. "I don't blame them for being shocked by the reality of war. It sucks, and no one should deny that. But the numbers of KIA attributed not just to Chris but to other snipers, and in fact other men during the combat, is largely a result of strategies aimed at reducing collateral damage and civilian fatalities in urban combat. So the reaction has always seemed to me more than a little ironic."

Kyle was less nuanced when he talked about it. He told people he wished he could somehow calculate the number of people he had saved. "That's the number I'd care about," he said. "I'd put that everywhere."

Taya always saw him as kind and loving, but "very principled." He would hold a door open for you, but if you didn't say thank you, he might slam it on you. "Chris, what if he just forgot to say thank you?" Taya would ask. "Well, I bet he won't forget next time," he'd say back. He would also wave to all of his neighbors. Most would wave back, except one man near their house in San Diego. "Where I'm from, neighbors wave," Kyle would say. Eventually he stopped waving to the man every time he saw him, and started flicking him off. "One way or the other, my hand is going up," he'd say.

Because of his firm principles, his strong black-and-white views of the world, the idea of war itself left him conflicted. He would often espouse the axiom "War is hell." But he also loved war. He didn't want to leave it. He would often say that staying home during a war is "a SEAL's worst nightmare."

While there were hundreds, probably thousands, of individuals he saved, the men who stayed most prominently in his memory long after the battles were over were the men he couldn't save. Losing his friends devastated him. When fellow Team 3 Charlie platoon member Marc Lee died in August of 2006 — the first SEAL to die in the Iraq War — Kyle was inconsolable. All of Lee's teammates prepared remarks for a memorial service in Ramadi. Kyle wrote out a speech, but when it came time to give it, he couldn't talk. Every time he tried, he broke down, sobbing.

"He came up and hugged me afterward," an active SEAL says. "He apologized. He said, 'I'm sorry. I wanted to, but I just couldn't do it.'"

It was at a similar event later that year — a wake for fallen SEAL Michael Monsoor, who was posthumously awarded the Medal of Honor for throwing himself on a grenade to save the lives of fellow SEALs — when Kyle reported having had his now-infamous confrontation with former Minnesota governor Jesse Ventura.

Kyle's story was in character: They were in a bar popular among SEALs in Coronado, California. Ventura, a former SEAL himself, was in town for an unrelated event and stopped by the wake. Ventura disrespected the troops, saying something to the effect of, "You guys deserve to lose a few." That was enough. Kyle punched him and left the bar.

Ventura denied the entire incident and filed a

lawsuit against Kyle, in which he has reportedly submitted sworn statements from several people saying that the incident never happened. Two other SEALs, friends of Kyle's, told me they were there that night and that it all happened just the way Kyle said it did.

One former SEAL, Andrew Paul, specifically asked to be on record saying, "This would be an excellent time for Mr. Ventura to do the right thing and drop his lawsuit."

Retired U.S. Navy SEAL Christopher Scott "Chris" Kyle stands in his home under the American flag. (Brandon Thibodeaux)

Chris Kyle sits for a portrait in his home outside of Dallas in March 2012. Kyle is known as the deadliest sniper in U.S. military history. (Brandon Thibodeaux)

Chris Kyle sits for a portrait in his home just two months after the release of his bestselling book. (Brandon Thibodeaux)

View from a camera perch moments before the funeral service of slain "American Sniper" Chris Kyle. (Photo courtesy of Jim Slaughter, 2013)

View from camera perch, just before Chris Kyle's funeral procession. (Flags for Chris Kyle © Jim Trahan)

Bagpiper plays "Amazing Grace" as the procession passes by.

Young girl and friend embrace as they look on at the funeral motorcade. (Photograph © Phillip G. Brown Fine Art Photography. All rights reserved. Used by permission)

Residents awaiting the procession where Texas State Highway 29 and Interstate 35 cross. (Photograph © Phillip G. Brown Fine Art Photography. All rights reserved. Used by permission.)

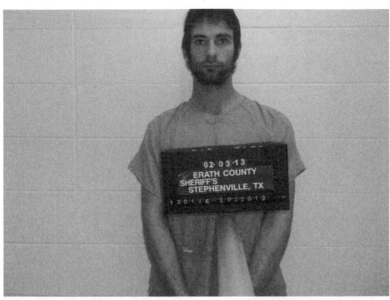

Eddie Ray Routh, twenty-five, was charged in connection with the murder of Navy SEAL Chris Kyle and his friend Chad Littlefield. (Erath County Police Department)

The front and back pages from the program at Chris Kyle's memorial ceremony. (Photographed by Tara Nieuwesteeg, 2013)

CHAPTER 9

BY 2009 THE life was taking its toll on Taya. She told Kyle that, because he was gone so much, she would see him just as often if she lived somewhere else. He took that as an ultimatum. As Kyle pointed out in his book and in interviews, the divorce rate among Navy SEALs is over 90 percent. He knew he wouldn't be able to do both anymore, to be a SEAL and a husband. So he left his promising career, the dream job for which he felt exceptionally well suited, the purpose that had kept him so motivated for ten years.

"When I first got out, I had a lot of resentment," he said. "I felt like she knew who I was when she met me. She knew I was a warrior.

That was all I'd ever wanted to do." He started drinking a lot. He stopped working out. He didn't want to leave the house or make his usual jokes. He missed the rush of combat, the way being at war sets your priorities straight. He missed knowing that what he was doing mattered. More than anything, though, he missed his brothers in the SEALs. He wrote to them and called them. He told people it felt like a daze.

The country was so much different in 2009 than it had been when the war began in 2003. He had been home during leave and between tours, but he was never back long enough to think about the cultural shifts. When he left for Iraq in 2003, it was still less than a year and a half after the attacks of September 11, 2001. The phrase "War on Terror" was ubiquitous, as were flag pins. Even Michael Moore was telling college students that they had to maintain respect for the troops. It seemed like every gas station sold those ribbon-shaped magnets meant to remind us to keep the military in our thoughts. There were giant American flags unrolled at so many football games, and patriotic songs filling huge chunks of the radio dial.

When the war began, there were protestors and many who opposed the war in this country (though almost none from any branch of the federal government), and a lot of those people were considered unpatriotic. More people were glued to their televisions, watching the war on cable news in near real time. This was a period when national magazines ran cover stories about the political power of American evangelicals and gay marriage was a wedge issue that helped conservatives, not liberals. Some people forget, George W. Bush was elected with a higher percentage of the vote in 2004 than he'd received in the previous election.

But just a few years later, things seemed so different. It felt like there was less unity than ever. The expression "War on Terror" was all but retired. And while there were still active military campaigns in two theaters, most of the country's attention was focused on the mushrooming financial crisis. There were more empty strip malls, more people looking for work, more Americans hurting.

In place of conservative political pundits, many news outlets hired either moderates or outspoken liberals. The country elected a president with "Hussein" right in his name. Now there were debates over gay marriage, legalizing pot, and the topic that got Kyle the most heated: gun control. The American public, and the rest of the world for that matter, had been besieged by images and stories such as those from Abu Ghraib, and public opinion had been swayed by the rising numbers of American casualties. The war in Iraq in particular had become extremely unpopular.

When Kyle wrote to his closest friends, he did talk about the one benefit of being out of the Navy. In all those years at war, he'd had almost no time with his two children. And in his time out, he discovered there was something he liked even more than being a cowboy or valiant sniper.

"He loved being a dad," Taya says. She noticed he could be rough and playful with their son and sweet and gentle with their daughter. "A lot of fathers play with their kids, but he was always on the floor with them, rolling around, making everyone giggle."

Kyle began to feel better. He got sick of feeling sorry for himself. He didn't want a divorce. He started working out again — "Getting my mind right," he called it.

When he met other vets who were feeling down, he told them they should try working out more, too. But many of them, especially the wounded men with prominent burns or missing limbs, explained that people stared too much. Gyms made them uncomfortable. That's how he got the idea to put gym equipment in the homes of veterans. When he approached FITCO — a company that provides exercise machines to gym facilities all over the country — and asked for any used equipment, they said no. Instead, they donated new equipment and helped fund a nonprofit dedicated to Kyle's mission.

This, more than anything, was what he wanted to show me, what he wanted people to read about. A lot of the men he met still struggled with the jarring trauma of their injuries. There was having to deal with injuries and missing appendages — in many cases, especially with wounds caused by IED attacks, men had what Kyle referred to as their "manhood" blown off — but there was also the abrupt disruption in their lives. As he described it, one minute they might be on a mission with their buddies, in the middle of combat somewhere in Iraq. The next thing they knew they were waking up in a hospital bed in Germany or Virginia, without certain body parts and without their closest friends. That detachment, the separation from their military brothers, was sometimes the worst part.

Then there was the struggle of dealing with the VA. (Even Kyle, The Legend, a man involved in six different explosions, was denied a disability claim.) There were the problems the men faced at home, with parents and children who didn't understand and spouses who weren't prepared for life with a disabled person.

But when Kyle would show up at a house with

brand-new exercise equipment — and he liked to deliver it himself whenever he had the chance — he could see people begin to change. Working out helped these men set goals. They could literally watch themselves getting stronger. Kyle was adamant about the program's effectiveness.

"It makes a real difference in these guys' lives," he said.

It wasn't immediate, but his new life had begun to come together.

"With helping people," Taya says, "Chris found his new purpose."

She watched him use the same willpower that had carried him through SEAL training and all those impossible missions, but now he was trying to become a better man. He started coaching his son's T-ball team and taking his daughter to dance practice. He'd always liked hunting, but he hated fishing. Still, when he learned that his son liked to fish, he dedicated himself to becoming a great fisherman so that they could bond the way he had with his own dad.

Kyle took the family to football games at Cowboys Stadium. (Once, when he had an extra ticket, he gave it to one of the building security guards at Craft and sat next to him through the whole game. "That's the kind of guy he was," Taya says.) He took them to church. Unless he was hanging out of a helicopter with a gun doing overwatch, he hated heights. But when his kids wanted to go, he took them to Six Flags to ride the roller coasters and to the State Fair for the Ferris wheel. His black truck became a familiar sight driving around Midlothian, where the family had settled.

He started collecting replicas of Old West guns, like the ones the cowboys used in movies he watched as a boy. Taya would find him practicing his quick draw and gun-twirling skills. Sometimes they would sit on the couch, watching TV, and he would twirl an unloaded six-shooter around his finger. If she saw someone on the screen that she didn't like, she would jokingly ask, "Can you shoot that guy?"

He'd point the pistol at the TV and pretend to fire.

"Got him, babe."

Taya always knew how special he was. Looking back, she's grateful for at least one particular moment not long before his death: They were in the living room. He was on the couch and she was up closing the blinds. Suddenly she stopped and stared at him. He looked up, confused.

"You know, I'm proud of you," she said. She told him she was proud of everything, of who he was as a person. "You're really incredible."

He began to turn the compliment around, to deflect as he always did. "Oh no, babe, you're the —"

She stopped him. "Just take it," she said. "I'm proud."

He looked at her, his bright eyes fixed on hers. "Thanks, babe."

CHAPTER 10

J. KYLE BASS is a hedge fund manager in Dallas, the founder of Hayman Capital Management. He was featured prominently in the Michael Lewis book *Boomerang: Travels in the New Third World,* which documented both Bass's keen financial mind and his fantastically opulent lifestyle. A few years ago, Bass was feeling overweight and out of shape. A former college athlete, he wanted something intense to get him back to his former self, so he found a Navy SEAL reserve commander in California, a man who gets prospective SEALs prepared for BUD/S training, and asked if they could tailor a short program for him. The commander obliged, and

Bass found that he really liked hanging out with the future and active SEALs. He said if they knew any SEALs coming back to Texas, he'd love to meet them.

That's how Bass met Chris Kyle. Bass was building a new house at the time, and he offered to fly Kyle in and pay him for some security consulting.

"I was just trying to come up with anything to help the guy out," Bass says. "I was looking for ways to try and help him make this transition back into the real world."

Bass invited Kyle to live at his house with him while Taya finished selling their place in San Diego. He introduced Kyle to as many "big money" people as he could. And the wealthy men were enthralled by Chris Kyle. They loved being around The Legend. They loved hearing his stories and invited him to lunch at expensive restaurants. Bass would hold an economic summit every year at his ranch in East Texas. He would kick off the festivities by introducing his sniper friends.

"I'd have Chris and other SEALs come out and do exhibition shoots," Bass says. "They would take six-hundred-yard shots at binary explosives, so when they hit them it's this giant explosion that shakes the ground." He smiles as he tells the story. "For all the people that manage money all over the world and on Wall Street to come to Texas and see a Navy SEAL sniper shoot a bomb, it's about as cool as it gets."

Bass and some business associates also helped start Craft International, and they brought Kyle on board as president. They put the Craft offices on the same floor as Hayman, so the finance folks and the defense contractors often crossed paths. Despite working in a plush office building in downtown Dallas, Kyle didn't change much. He'd walk through the doors in his jeans, boots, and ball cap. Even if he saw an important meeting, it wouldn't stop him from grinning and flicking off the entire room of people. Once, Kyle walked into a coworker's office and announced he was giving the man a raise. Then he slapped his big hand down on the man's desk and lifted it up to reveal a shiny new penny. Kyle grinned at his own joke.

He also brought with him his affinity for doling out his special "hugs." One time, late at night during a company retreat, Kyle was playing poker with the guys. One of the in-house attorneys who had a bit too much to drink that night thought it would be funny to mess with Kyle. When Kyle's little boy would do something to elicit a reaction, Taya used to call it "poking the bear." This night, during the poker game, the attorney was most certainly poking the bear.

Bass recalls the attorney walked by Kyle and playfully flipped the cap off of the sniper's head. Everyone laughed and there were several "ohhhh" reactions from surprised onlookers. Kyle only smiled, though, and continued playing. He was nearly twice the lawyer's size, and the guy was drunk. He let it slide. But when it happened again, Kyle jumped up, grinning, and chased the man down. Within seconds he caught him and was putting him gently to sleep on the floor.

As one friend puts it, "It was funny, unless it was happening to you."

The business concept behind Craft was to market Kyle's other skills. His credentials when it came to things like close-combat proficiency, marksmanship, and heavy-artillery training were as good as they come. He would be able to help train troops (a lot of military training is done by third-party contractors), police officers, and wealthy businessmen who would pay top dollar for hands-on instruction from an elite warrior such as Chris Kyle. It was fun, but more important to him, he felt that by training police officers and defense contractors working in America's interests, he was still contributing something to the fight. If he couldn't be in the middle of the action himself, he figured, he could make sure the people who were had the best preparation possible.

He did a lot of his training at Rough Creek Lodge in Glen Rose, a luxury resort with an extended shooting range. It's the same place he would take buddies and wounded vets when they were feeling down and needed to unwind. He said a lot of people didn't understand, but when you're on your stomach, aiming at targets hundreds of yards away, it's actually a little peaceful. You have to be still. You have to control your breathing and block out any thoughts that don't pertain to the goal at hand. In some ways, it's as close as someone like Chris Kyle came to meditating.

CHAPTER 11

WHEN CARLOS HATHCOCK was in Vietnam, someone gave him a scrap of paper with something scribbled on it. By the time he got out of the Marines, he didn't carry the piece of paper with him anymore because he had the words memorized. It was a quote attributed to Ernest Hemingway: "There is no hunting like the hunting of a man, and those who have hunted armed men long enough and liked it, never care for anything else thereafter."

Chris Kyle didn't feel that way at all. From the time he was a boy, he had loved going out into nature, hunting with friends or family. Once he was back from the war, he rarely turned down an invitation to a deer lease. (On a lease, a hunter pays a landowner with a deer crossing on his or her property for the right to hunt there. These are common in Texas.) Many of the wealthy businessmen who befriended him also invited him to their ranches.

One year, after Kyle Bass's economic summit, one of Bass's longtime friends, a man who also invests with Hayman Capital, invited the legendary sniper to go hunting with a small group of finance guys on his ranch. This investor friend is, in the crude parlance of Texas businessmen, a "deer queer" — someone who breeds deer and thinks of the animals a little like pets. Throughout his property, there are several large binders full of pictures of deer. There's one in the living room of the main house, and there are binders in each of the deer blinds set up around the ranch. Each binder has large full-color photos of all the deer on the property. And there are two lists, some deer you can shoot, and some deer you can't.

Kyle was out in one of the deer blinds around

dusk when he saw something move on the horizon. He saw a tall, heavy rack in the distance. He started flipping through the binder of deer, trying to match what he could see to one of the photos so he knew which list the deer was on.

Because it was getting dark, Kyle was having a hard time seeing. He also didn't want to have his nose in the binder while the animal wandered off. Finally he found a picture of the deer, and it was on the "OK to shoot" list — or so he thought. It was getting late, so Kyle lined up his rifle and — boom. He dropped the deer in one shot.

As the shots echoed around the property, the host put a call out over the radio. Which deer had been shot?

Kyle took another look at the animal in the distance, and another look at the binder, and he concluded he had killed a deer named 8 Ball. He said so over the radio.

So the host, a powerful businessman, drove his buggy over to that part of the ranch. He stopped at the deer, lying right where Kyle had killed it. The host got out of the vehicle and walked over to the animal. Without saying a single word, the man got back into the buggy, drove to his car, and drove to Dallas.

As it turned out, Kyle hadn't killed 8 Ball. He had killed the man's prize breeding buck, worth tens of thousands of dollars. The deer was named En Fuego because his wide rack had the rare colorings of a blazing campfire.

Soon Bass got wind of what had happened on the ranch. He's been friends with this man since college, and as college buddies tend to do, they've often teased each other over the years. So Bass couldn't resist the opportunity. He called his friend.

"I just said, 'Hey, I heard Chris was *en fuego* at your ranch this weekend,'" Bass says. "He gave me an eff you and hung up the phone and didn't talk to anyone for a couple of weeks."

When Kyle realized what he'd done, he felt bad. In an effort to make things right, he offered the man his .338 rifle, the gun he had carried in-theater, a weapon that will almost certainly end up in a museum one day. The businessman was overwhelmed by the gesture. More than touched, he declined the offer. Instead, the man is having a bronze statue of the deer made, to stand in that spot. There will be a small placard that will read "Shaitan."

"Now," says Bass, "it's folklore."

CHAPTER 12

KYLE INSISTED THAT he never had any intention of writing a book. But Scott McEwen, an attorney in San Diego, had heard many of the legendary tales involving Kyle and thought they needed to be collected in one place. Soon he was put in touch with HarperCollins publishers and the New York writer Jim DeFelice. Kyle figured if it was going to happen regardless, he might as well participate. He wanted to give credit where he felt it was due. Ultimately, he decided that the book would provide an opportunity to tell the stories of his SEAL brothers.

"If it was going to be done anyway," he said, "it might as well be done right."

Technically, he started the process before he officially agreed to put his name on the book. He and Taya were flown to New York in the middle of winter to meet DeFelice and begin pouring out their story. It was supposed to work a little like an oral history: DeFelice would ask questions, and all Kyle would have to do was answer them. Then the writer would record the stories as best he could in Kyle's voice and words. But the interviews were exhausting.

"He was not naturally loquacious," DeFelice says. "Nor did he particularly like to talk about himself. When we first started working together, telling me what happened in the war put an enormous strain on him. He was reliving battles in great detail for the first time since he'd gotten out of the service. He could have been killed in any number of the situations he'd been in. That's a reality that can be difficult to comprehend at the time, and even harder to understand later on."

Kyle did find time at one point for a snowball fight with DeFelice's thirteen-year-old son. The war hero claimed he'd had plenty of experience in snow, but on this day, the boy got the better of him. Kyle came running in and grabbed a beer.

"Okay, kid," Kyle told him. "Now you can say you beat a Navy SEAL in a snowball fight."

The writing process seemed to wear on the war hero. "His dad told me later that Chris looked like he'd been through hell after the first long weekend we worked together," DeFelice says. "I can't recall his exact words, but it was clear that the work had taken a huge amount out of him."

DeFelice noticed that, gradually, talking about his experiences became easier for Kyle.

"Hopefully, telling the story put the pressure of the war into some sort of manageable perspective," he says. "I think he got more comfortable talking about things. He eventually reached a point where he could see his war experiences as an important part of his life, but not as *everything* in his life. I think the danger he'd been in started, not necessarily to fade, but to become more manageable and objective."

DeFelice adds, "I think Taya, the family, and his close friends were all a big part of that. I think it helped, too, that he came to see the book as a way to help not just the families of the two men who'd died next to him, but all service people in general. Not help in a big way, just help them by telling other people what they'd been through."

Kyle decided not to take a dime from *American Sniper*. As it became a bestseller, his share amounted to more than $1.5 million. He said he gave two-thirds to the families of fallen teammates and the rest to a charity that helped wounded veterans. It was something he and Taya discussed a lot.

"I would ask him, 'How much is enough? Where does your family fit in?'" she says. "But I understood."

When the book came out in early 2012, everyone wanted to interview him. He was on late-night talk shows, cable news, and radio. He did a number of reality TV shows related to shooting. (He rarely took much money from the appearances.) He always went on with a ball cap on his head and a wad of tobacco in his mouth.

There are stories of people trying to put makeup on him backstage. A pleasant, sweet woman from the network would approach him with the case of cosmetics.

"Nope," he would say.

"But everyone on TV wears it," producers or offended makeup artists would reply.

"Not gonna happen."

His favorite appearance — or at least his friends' favorite — was on Conan O'Brien's show. The comedian was in good form that night, and rarely did Kyle laugh so loudly or smile so much in public. The interview began with O'Brien complimenting him on the early success of the book. Then he asked about SEAL Team 6, the team made famous after the raid that killed Osama Bin Laden.

"What's the difference between SEAL Team 3 and SEAL Team 6?" the host asked.

Kyle, wearing boots, jeans, a black collared shirt bearing the Craft logo, and a ball cap, answered in his slow Texas drawl. "Well," he said. "Originally you had SEAL Team 1 and SEAL Team 2. And then they formed up a special unit that was called SEAL Team 6. Since then, so many guys have been coming in — we've been building up the forces — that they started filling in the rest of the numbers. To go from one of the other SEAL teams to 6, you basically have to go through another boot camp and tryout."

O'Brien asked if he'd wanted to be in SEAL Team 6.

"At the time I did not," Kyle said, earnest. "But looking back at it, yes, I wish I would have."

"You've got an amazing story," O'Brien said. "You've got nothing to be ashamed of. But it might be fun to walk into a bar now and go 'SEAL Team 6!'" The host pointed at himself with both thumbs, emphasizing his own smarminess. "I do that a lot."

Kyle might have been a bit nervous at first, but now he erupted with laughter. O'Brien rolled with it. "I tell people I was on that raid," he said. "And no one believes it. Then I give details that just aren't, you know — we got him in Baltimore!"

The host asked about Kyle's longest shot. "Twenty-one football fields away," O'Brien said. "I can't even understand making a shot from that distance."

Without missing a beat, Kyle chimed in, "I can't either." The audience howled with laughter.

"It was an accident," O'Brien joked. "You dropped your rifle." The crowd kept the laughs coming.

Then the host asked about the level of technology employed by modern snipers, and how different sniping was in the past.

"I definitely cheated," Kyle said. By now the two of them seemed to feed off each other. They shared real comedic timing. "I just use a ballistic computer that tells me everything to do. So I'm just a monkey on a gun."

"I wouldn't go that far," O'Brien said.

Throughout the short interview, Kyle, the mannered Texan he was, kept calling O'Brien *sir*.

"You don't have to call me *sir*, by the way," O'Brien quipped. "I'm a talk show host."

Afterward, Kyle's friends would note how comfortable he eventually seemed, how nice it was to have the world see him laugh like they had so many times.

He also did appearances at churches. On Fourth of July weekend in 2012, he went to Fellowship Church in Grapevine, Texas, one of the largest mega-churches in the country. (There are five "campuses" spread between Texas and Florida, and the sermons are broadcast and streamed to tens of thousands more around the world.) The pastor, Ed Young, introduced him to the audience by explaining that while all too often "we forget what we should remember and remember what we forget," a Christian should always keep in mind the sacrifices made by the people who secure our freedom with their blood. He called Kyle "a guest who is maybe the best we have ever had in the history of our church."

Kyle came out on stage wearing his jeans, boots, T-shirt, and hat, but this time he was sans tobacco. Though he sometimes complained about how he didn't enjoy church as a boy, he also told people what a proud Christian he'd been his entire life. His duty to God, he explained, was the only thing that came before his responsibilities to his country and family. He was comfortable in church. He sat relaxed in a plush white chair across from the pastor. Young, an author of many books himself, explained that he hadn't read *American Sniper* yet because "I didn't want the book to taint what we were going to talk about."

"I'm glad you didn't read it, either," Kyle said, grinning. "There's bad words in there."

They talked about how he became a SEAL, how in training SEALs treated everyone, both officers and enlisted, as equals, as teammates working toward a goal. They talked about the values of giving your life to pay for the freedom of others, self-sacrifice in the name of strangers. "If you want to go protest," Kyle said, "it's been paid for you to go do that."

Young pointed out that there were parallels

between the way people "trample over the blood" of both Jesus and military personnel.

"But in no way are we like Jesus," Kyle said. The audience snickered. "Don't compare me too much to him."

They talked about how important it is to submit to and respect authority — "even the people you don't like," Kyle said. "If it's someone in some certain position, you don't have to respect the person, but you *will* respect that position. And you will *show* respect. The only way you get it is by earning it, and that's by showing it."

Kyle had 1,200 people at his first public book signing. It was similar in every town. He preferred to stand for the length of the book signings. "If y'all are standing, I can stand," he said. He would wait until he signed every book he was asked to, even if it took hours. It often did, because he wanted to take a moment to talk with each person. He tried to personalize each book. He'd pose for photos, one after another.

As he became more famous, more people

wanted to spend time with him. More politicians wanted to go shooting with him. At one point, he was at a range with Governor Rick Perry. Perry was about to shoot the sniper rifle and asked Kyle if he had an extra pad to put on the cement before he lay down. Kyle replied with a mock-serious tone. "You know, Governor," he said, "Ann Richards was out here not too far back, and she didn't need a pad at all."

A good friend once introduced him to the movie star Natalie Portman. He asked her what she did for a living. And, as the story goes, she liked him even more after that.

Then there is this story: Kyle had been invited to a luxury suite at a University of Texas football game and decided to take a heartbroken buddy of his, a Dallas police officer who had recently caught his girlfriend making out with another guy. They were in the suite for a few hours, talking and drinking, when a former Texas football star happened to walk in. At some point Kyle realized that this former star was also the guy who had kissed his friend's girlfriend.

Kyle's friend knew what was coming. He begged him not to, but it was in vain.

"It's man law," Kyle said.

Sure enough, Kyle approached the former star and gave him a "hug" right there in the suite. As women were shrieking and wondering if the former football great was dead, Kyle kept the hold for just a little longer than usual, causing the man to lose control of his bowels as he passed out.

It wasn't just his friends he took care of. People wrote to him from all over the world, asking for favors or for his time, especially after he started appearing on TV. He did his best to accommodate every request he could, even when Taya was worried he was spreading himself too thin.

"He was so trusting," she says. "He didn't let himself worry about much."

CHAPTER 13

JODI ROUTH REACHED out to Kyle because she knew his history of caring for veterans and thought he might be able to help her son. Kyle told people he and his friend Chad Littlefield were going to take the kid out to blow off some steam.

Littlefield was a buddy Kyle had come to count on over the past few years. They met as dads on the T-ball field. Littlefield would come over at 5:00 a.m. sometimes to work out with his friend. Often they could sit for hours and never talk, totally comfortable in silence. It became a joke between Taya and her husband.

"Well, Chad and I were real chatty this morning," Kyle would say, and Taya would laugh. "Oh yeah?" she would say back. "Ya'll say one sentence, or two?"

Littlefield had come over a few nights earlier to have Kyle adjust the scope of his rifle. Littlefield brought a bag from Sonic and two tall drinks. As he stood there that night, with Kyle working on the gun, Littlefield looked up at Taya, smiling.

That night Kyle invited Littlefield to come with him to Rough Creek. They were going to take Jodi Routh's son shooting. Littlefield had accompanied Kyle on similar trips dozens of times.

They were in Kyle's big black truck when they showed up in the Dallas suburb of Lancaster, at the home Eddie Ray Routh shared with his parents. The Rouths hoped time with a war hero, a legend like Chris Kyle, might help their son.

It was a little after lunchtime on Saturday, February 2, when they picked up Routh and headed west on Route 67. Kyle drove right past the exit for his own house, past the waving Texas flags along the highway. The threesome went through one small town after another, past high schools and police stations and any number of gas stations. The drive took about an hour and a half. They got to Rough Creek Lodge around 3:15 p.m. They turned up a snaking three-mile road toward the lodge and let a Rough Creek employee know they were heading to the range, another mile and a half down a rocky, unpaved road.

This was a place Kyle loved. He had given many lessons here over the past three years. He'd spend hours working with anyone who showed an interest in shooting. This is where he would take his boys when they needed to get away. In the right light, the dry, blanched hills and cliffs looked a little like the places he'd been to in Iraq. When a group of vets went out there, away from the rest of the world, they could re-lax and enjoy the camaraderie so many of them missed.

We may never know exactly what happened

next. They weren't there long, police suspect, before Routh turned his semiautomatic pistol on Kyle and Littlefield. He took Kyle's truck, left Rough Creek, and headed east on 67. Later he would tell his sister that he "traded his soul for a new truck." Less than two hours after the three men first pulled through the lodge's front gate, a hunting guide from the lodge spotted two bodies covered in blood, both shot multiple times.

Routh drove to a friend's house in Alvarado and called his sister. Then he drove to her house, where, his sister told police, he was "out of his mind." He told her he'd murdered two people, that he'd shot them "before they could kill him." He said "people were sucking his soul" and that he could "smell the pigs." She told him he needed to turn himself in.

From there, Routh drove home to Lancaster, where the police were waiting for him. When they tried to talk him out of the truck, he sped off. With the massive grill guard, he ripped through the front of a squad car. They chased

Routh through Lancaster and into Dallas. He was headed north on I-35 when the motor of Kyle's truck finally burned out, near Wheatland Road. Routh was arrested and charged with two counts of murder.

CHAPTER 14

THE MEMORIAL WAS held a little more than a week after the murders. Marcus Luttrell and his wife, Melanie, along with a number of Kyle's family friends, coordinated the events. There were no buildings in Midlothian that could accommodate the thousands of people who wanted to be there. Jerry Jones offered up Cowboys Stadium, an arena Kyle had marveled over before his death. There would be a small, private service for friends and family, then a larger one open to the public.

Messages spread through social media. Press releases went out to local outfits. Several national outlets, including the *New York Times* and *Time* magazine, sent reporters. Nobody knew exactly how many people to expect.

There were no vendors in the parking lot that day. There was nobody selling parking. A few TV news vans parked at various entry points, where the cameras could pick up the streams of mourners or packs of police motorcycles.

Celebrities came, including Jerry Jones, Troy Aikman, and Sarah Palin. Hundreds of motorcycle riders lined the outside of the field. Bagpipe players and drummers came from all over the state. A military choir stood at the ready the entire time.

A stage was set up in the middle of the football field. On the stage stood a podium, a few microphone stands, some speakers. At the front of the stage, amid a mound of flowers, were Kyle's gun, his boots, his body armor, and his helmet.

The funeral programs were printed in color. On the front, imposed over a waving American flag, was a picture of Kyle standing next to a pickup truck, grinning. In the photo, he's wearing a cowboy hat and sunglasses. He also has a pistol tucked into his belt and two bandoliers strapped across his chest. On the back of the program was a picture of Kyle and Taya on their wedding day and a picture of Kyle's rifle. Below that there were handwritten notes from each of his children.

"Daddy," the first one read. "I love you, Dad. You are the best dad ever. I never wanted you to die. I will miss your heart. I will love you even if you died. Love you forever, Baby Girl."

The second one, from his son, read, "I miss you a lot. One of the best things that has happened to me is you. I love you, Dad. I always will. Love, Bubba."

Photos from Kyle's life scrolled by on the gigantic screen overhead. There he was as a boy, getting a shotgun for Christmas. There he was as a young cowboy, riding a horse. Then, as a newly inducted SEAL, clean shaven and bright eyed. In combat, scanning for targets. In the desert, flying a Texas flag. With his platoon, a fearsome image of American might. At home, hugging Taya, kissing the foot of his baby girl, holding the hand of his little boy.

Even before the ceremony started, there were a few damp eyes. Chris Kyle inspired people. The stories of his life transcended things like age, race, and political affiliation. For these people, he stood for something important. He was an icon who exemplified the times he lived in.

His casket was draped with the American flag and placed on the giant star at the fifty-yard line.

Randy Travis played "Whisper My Name" and "Amazing Grace." Joe Nichols played "The Impossible." Kyle's friend Scott Brown told a story about how they contemplated buying a bar one day and how the sniper decided the perfect name for the place would be Valor. Then Brown played a song he wrote by the same name.

The public heard stories about what Kyle was like as a little boy. What he was like in training. What he was like at war. What he was like as a friend and business partner. Some people talked about the times they saw him cry. Fellow SEALs told stories about his resolve, his humor, his bravery. There were tales of his compassion, his intelligence, his dedication to God.

"Though we feel sadness and loss," one of his former commanders said, "know this: legends never die. Chris Kyle is not gone. Chris Kyle is everywhere. He is the fabric of the freedom that blessed the people of this great nation. He is forever embodied in the strength and tenacity of the SEAL teams, where his courageous path will be followed and his memory is enshrined as SEALs continue to ruthlessly hunt down and destroy America's enemies."

Aside from a few brief patriotism-inspired outbursts, the crowd was ghostly silent. Though there were nearly ten thousand people in attendance, you could hear individual footsteps on the field. You could hear the quivering in each voice.

A young sailor stood on stage and thanked Kyle's parents for raising him the way they did. Then the young man read a letter the parents had written for the memorial.

"A parent's love is forever," the letter began. "We shared Chris's laughter, his smile, his pranks, his jokes, and his stories. Always a story to be told, and only in the way Chris could express so vividly." The letter addressed Kyle directly and spoke eloquently of his parents' belief that their son had a purpose on this planet. "God anointed you with the name Protector," his parents wrote. "Your life embodied the full meaning of that. You were tender to the young, compassionate with the wounded, and sympathetic for the less fortunate. The Lord had his hand on you from the moment you were born. You were destined for greatness."

Taya stood strong, surrounded by her husband's SEAL brothers, and told the world about their love. Jeff Kyle stood next to her on stage in his crisp Marine uniform. Just days earlier, Jeff's wife had given birth to a baby girl. She was due on March 5, but arrived early — in time to meet her Uncle Chris before he died. At one point, as Taya eulogized her husband and broke down in tears, Jeff offered her a white glove from his hand.

She made sure to talk about Chad Littlefield,

and what a great friend he'd been to her husband. "In the craziness of life, Chad came along with his quiet, large presence and an easy smile, complete with a rugged beard and dimples, and blessed Chris with a friendship," she said. "That was the one thing Chris needed more than anything."

She talked a bit about the tumult of their relationship. "I don't need to romanticize Chris," she said. "Because our reality is messy, passionate, full of every extreme emotion known to man, including fear, compassion, anger, pain, laughing so hard we doubled over and hugged it out, laughing when we were irritated with each other, and laughing when we were so in love it felt like someone hung the moon for only us."

She stopped to wipe her face with Jeff's glove and spoke to her children in words beautifully pitched for their ears. "My sweet angels, we will put one foot in front of the other and remember how silly Dad was. We will hug each other tightly just like Dad would do with us. We will pray the prayers he prayed with us. We will remember that your dad has so much pride in your manners, your good sportsmanship, and your friendship to each other, and we will continue them all. We will remember that his Baby Girl and his Bubba mean the world to him and he didn't just talk about that. He loved you, and he lived his life to show you."

Then, in front of thousands of people, reporters from all over the globe, and a slew of cameras, she spoke directly to her husband.

"God knew it would take the toughest and softest-hearted man on earth to get a hardheaded, cynical, hard-loving woman like me to see what God needed me to see, and he chose you for the job," she said, her cracking voice filling the stadium. She spoke of how he taught her to love, to have faith, to be independent, to raise their children with respect and old-fashioned values, and even to curb her anger. Before continuing her list, she added as to that last item: "By the way, sorry that took so long."

Before leaving the stage, she looked at the casket on the fifty-yard line. Through the tears, she said, "I love you, Chris. I love you. I love you."

When the ceremony ended, uniformed pall-bearers carried out the casket to the sounds of mournful bagpipes. Taya walked behind them with her children, hand in hand.

The next day, the casket was driven to Austin. There was a procession nearly two hundred miles long — the Department of Public Safety says it was almost certainly the longest in American history. People lined the road in every town, waving flags and saluting. American flags were draped over every single bridge on I-35 between the Kyle home in Midlothian and the state capital.

As the family and friends drove for hours through the rain, the line of people along the highway never stopped. Thousands of people stood there, cold and wet, happy to do it. There were men in suits standing next to men in over-alls. There were little girls with pigtails, their cheeks painted red, white, and blue. There were parents, pointing out the hero to their children as the casket drove by.

He was laid to rest in the Texas State Cemetery in Austin, rarefied grounds for any Texan. He could have been buried in Arlington National Cemetery, with all the pomp and circumstance that comes with it. But that isn't what he would have wanted. Jeff told reporters that, if it had been up to his brother, he'd be fine being buried beneath an old oak tree in a pasture somewhere.

Kyle didn't want to be remembered as the sniper, or The Legend, his brother said. "He just wanted to be known as Chris Kyle."

CHAPTER 15

PEOPLE WILL TELL stories about Chris Kyle for generations to come. Tales of his feats in battle, and of his antics and noble deeds, will probably swell. In a hundred years, people won't know which stories are completely true and which were embellished over time. And, in the end, it may not matter too much because people believe in legends for all their own reasons.

Since her husband's death, Taya has been overwhelmed by the number of veterans who want to tell her that Chris Kyle saved their lives. A man with a two-year-old girl wept recently as he explained that his daughter would not have been born had it not been for Chris Kyle rescuing him in Iraq. Years from now, men will still be telling stories about the moments when they were seconds or inches from death, when they thought it was all over — only to have a Chris Kyle bullet fly from the heavens and take out their enemies. They'll tell their grandchildren to thank Chris Kyle in their prayers.

Because his legend is so large, because he personally protected so many people, there will surely be men who think they were saved by Kyle but who owe their lives to a different sniper or to another serviceman. Of course, there will be no way to know for sure. Kyle credited his SEAL brothers any chance he could, but he also knew that he was an American hero, the most accomplished sniper the country has had, and he knew the complications that came with that reputation.

During the interview in which he discussed the gas station incident, he didn't say where it happened. Most versions of the story have him in Cleburne, not far from Fort Worth. The Cleburne police chief says that if such an incident did happen, it wasn't in his town. Every other chief of police along Route 67 says the same thing. Public information requests produced no police reports, no coroner reports, nothing from the Texas Rangers or the Department of Public Safety. I stopped at every gas station along 67, Business 67 in Cleburne, and ten miles in either direction. Nobody had heard of anything like that happening.

A lot of people will believe that, because there are no public documents or witnesses to corroborate his story, Kyle must have been lying. But why would he lie? He was already one of the most decorated veterans of the Iraq War. Tales of his heroism on the battlefield were already lore in every branch of the armed forces.

People who never met Kyle will think there must have been too much pressure on him, a war hero who thought he might seem purposeless if he wasn't killing bad guys. Conspiracy theorists will wonder if maybe every part of his life story—his incredible kills, his heroic tales of bravery in the face of death—was concocted by the propaganda wing of the Pentagon.

And, of course, other people — probably most people — will believe the story because it is about Chris Kyle. He was one of the few men in the entire world capable of such a feat. He was one of the only people alive who might have had the connections to make something like that disappear (he did work regularly with the CIA). People will believe it because Chris Kyle was incredible, the most celebrated war hero of our time, a true American hero in every sense of the word. They'll believe this story because there are already so many verified stories of his lethal abilities and astonishing valor, stories of him hanging out with presidents, ribbing governors, and knocking out bullies and former football stars and billionaires and cocky frat boys.

They'll believe it because Chris Kyle is already a legend, and sometimes we need to believe in legends.

EPILOGUE

January 2015

AND THE LEGEND continues to grow. The first trailer for *American Sniper* surfaced in October 2014, more than two months before the film was released. It opens with the clicking of a rifle. Then we see Chris Kyle, played by Bradley Cooper, perched on a roof, ball cap on backward, providing overwatch as a tank slowly hums past and American troops go door-to-door through a tattered Iraqi village. Then a man of military age appears through the scope of Kyle's rifle. The man is watching the American convoy, talking on a cell phone, before darting out of sight. Soon a woman and a child come out of a doorway nearby, heading for the Americans on the ground. Cooper, as Kyle, quickly surmises that the woman is carrying a Russian grenade and sees her hand it to the child. We see flashbacks to other parts of the sniper's life. We see his marriage. We see the birth of his son. We see him playing with his little girl. We see him sitting next to flag-draped coffins. As the dramatic music builds, as the child carries the grenade ever closer to the convoy, we hear someone tell him: "They fry you if you're wrong."

Then it cuts to black.

In less than two minutes, we witness the moral dilemma of a sniper, the moral quagmire created by this war. We see an American struggling at home, a wife torn apart by the life she and her husband are living. We see a terse, tense piece of cinema, truncated in a way that mirrors the life story of the title character.

Kyle was a phenomenon before he was discharged from the Navy. People in every branch of the United States Armed Forces had heard tales of him. When his autobiography came out in 2012, the Chris Kyle phenomenon grew. His name climbed the bestseller lists, and for anyone looking, it seemed like he was everywhere. He was on Fox News, on TBS, on C-SPAN, on several different radio shows. He went to festivals and conferences. He did interviews with both national and regional newspapers and magazines.

When he died, the shocking news brought even more people to his story. They bought his book. Over the next weeks and months, they scoured the internet for videos and interviews and profiles. They read blogs about things he'd said and done. Some tried to psychoanalyze him from afar, debating whether he really was a hero. Most mourned his loss and grieved for his friends, his family, his teammates, and his nation.

But when that first movie trailer was released, people familiar with Chris Kyle's story knew: this phenomenon was just beginning. The film didn't get the kind of thoughtful attention some of the other award-season releases received. There weren't a lot of ads in most markets. There wasn't a single Golden Globe nomination. There was more buzz for *Selma* and *Foxcatcher* and *Birdman* and *The Imitation Game.* There was infinitely more talk about the Seth Rogen–James Franco–North Korea comedy, *The Interview.*

On Christmas Day, *American Sniper* was released in New York, Los Angeles, and Dallas, and it started breaking records immediately. First the movie broke the record for limited Christmas releases. Then it broke individual theater records. Then, when it was released nationally, it broke records for both January and R-rated openings. That weekend the movie earned more money than the next ten movies combined did. Within two weeks, it had brought in more than two hundred million dollars. These are numbers traditionally associated with superhero movies.

The story quickly soaked into our culture, into our social and political debate. The words *American Sniper* — and indeed the name Chris Kyle — became something of a Rorschach test. Commentators up and down the dial and on what felt like every blog weighed in on the various developing storylines. Celebrities all across the political spectrum posted their thoughts. For a few days, it seemed like the entire internet had morphed into a factory that cranked out nothing but *American Sniper* think pieces.

There were questions about his language, about his lack of remorse, and about the veracity of his stories — about the 1.8 million dollars a Minnesota jury awarded Jesse Ventura, a verdict that might have gone the other way had the trial taken place in Texas. There were debates over the quality of the movie, talk about how Bradley Cooper prepared for the role (he put on fifty pounds of muscle and hired a coach to help him with the Texas accent), and theories about potential subtexts director Clint Eastwood may have been trying to work in. There was a substantial amount of attention paid to the fake baby used in one dramatic scene.

Some individuals — many of whom were opposed to the war in Iraq to begin with, or generally object to gun culture and a lot of the conservative beliefs Kyle was associated with — would rather sweep away the positive notions about him. They don't want to believe that anyone who could have said or done the things he said and did could have helped anyone. They talk about bloodlust and cowardice.

There are also some people who believe he could do no wrong. They'd like to simplify him into a totemic icon. They'd like to think that heroes are infallible or that heroism isn't subjective.

Of course, both views are problematic. He was much more than a two-hour movie. He was a complicated human being. He was a killer and he was a victim. He was both incredibly brutal and incredibly loving. He was kind and provocative and playful. A few things are certain, no matter what you think of the wars, or of Chris Kyle himself: He did save American lives. He did help countless veterans at home. The movie has exposed a lot of Americans to the ravages of war and the toll war takes on families. And his story is anything but simple.

Taya Kyle may have summed it up best at her

husband's funeral. "I'm not a fan of people romanticizing their loved ones in death," she said. "I don't need to romanticize Chris. Because our reality is messy, passionate, full of every extreme emotion known to man."

ACKNOWLEDGMENTS

Every step of this project was a collaboration. Every person involved played an important role. Thank you to everyone who was kind to me, in either a personal or professional capacity, while I was reporting, writing, and editing. I know it's not easy for the people around me, and for that I'm sorry.

I'm especially grateful to Taya Kyle for being so unbelievably kind and understanding, and to all of Chris's friends who took the time to share their stories with me. While the world lost a hero, you lost so much more.

This book would not have been possible if not for the following people: Tim Rogers, Zac Crain, Krista Nightengale, Wick Allison, Halley Homen, and everyone else at *D Magazine;* David

Patterson and Anissa Stocks at Foundry + Media; John Parsley, Ben Allen, Malin von Euler-Hogan, and Marie Mundaca at Little, Brown; Elisa Rivlin; Brandon Thibodeaux, one of the finest photographers in the country; and George Getschow at the Mayborn, to whom I will always owe beer.

Above all, I am thankful to all the men and women who have dedicated their lives to keeping the rest of us safe and free enough to do things like read and write books.

ABOUT THE AUTHOR

Michael J. Mooney is a staff writer at *D Magazine*. He also writes for *GQ*, *ESPN The Magazine*, *Outside*, and *Grantland*. He is a graduate of the Mayborn School of Journalism, and is on the advisory committee of the Mayborn Literary Nonfiction Conference. His stories have appeared in *The Best American Crime Reporting* and multiple editions of *The Best American Sports Writing*. He lives in Dallas with his fiancée, Tara, and their retired racing greyhound.

THE LIFE AND LEGEND OF CHRIS KYLE